Made in United States
Troutdale, OR
11/10/2023

14461696R00070